LIVE 100 YEARS HAPPILY

TRANSFORM YOUR LIFE WITH JAPANESE TECHNIQUES

ASHISH SINGH

BlueRose ONE.com
Stories Matter

Title: LIVE 100 YEARS HAPPILY
Language: English
Character set encoding: UTF-8
First published by

BlueRose ONE.com
Stories Matter

An Imprint of BlueRose Publishers

Head Office: B-6, 2nd Floor,
ABL Workspaces, Block B, Sector 4,
Noida, Uttar Pradesh 201301
M: +91-8882 898 898

BlueRose ONE .com
Stories Matter

PREFACE

In today's fast-paced world, we are often caught in the whirlwind of constant change, pressure to succeed, and an unrelenting quest for perfection. In the midst of this, I found myself drawn to the wisdom of Japanese culture, where simplicity, patience, and an appreciation for the imperfect hold significant value. My journey to Japan, both physically and spiritually, revealed to me a treasure trove of principles that are not only timeless but also profoundly applicable to our modern lives.

This book is a culmination of my experiences, learnings, and reflections during my years in Japan. Each chapter delves into a Japanese principle that has the potential to transform the way we live, work, and perceive the world around us. From the concept of Ikigai, which guides us in finding our purpose, to Kaizen, which teaches us the power of continuous improvement, these principles are interwoven with practical advice and personal anecdotes to offer a holistic approach to personal development.

In writing this book, I have drawn upon not only my experiences but also the wisdom shared with me by friends, mentors, and colleagues in Japan. Their insights have been invaluable in shaping my understanding of these principles and their application in daily life.

As you turn the pages of this book, I hope you find inspiration and practical guidance to embark on your own journey of self-discovery and growth. Whether you are seeking balance, fulfillment, or simply a new perspective on life, the principles shared here are meant to be a source of guidance and encouragement.

This book is not a manual to be followed step by step but rather a companion that you can turn to whenever you need a gentle reminder of the beauty of simplicity, the power of patience, and the value of embracing life's imperfections.

I invite you to explore these principles with an open heart and mind, and to apply them in a way that resonates with your unique journey. May this book serve as a beacon of light, guiding you toward a more fulfilling and meaningful life.

With gratitude and humility,

Ashish Singh

PROLOGUE

In a world that constantly demands more—more speed, more efficiency, more perfection—we often find ourselves yearning for less. Less chaos. Less noise. Less pressure to keep up with the relentless pace of life. It is within this longing for simplicity that the wisdom of Japanese culture finds its relevance and resonance.

This book is not a prescription, nor a step-by-step guide to success or happiness. Instead, it is an invitation—a gentle nudge to pause, reflect, and embrace a way of living that values balance over excess, progress over perfection, and harmony over haste.

Inspired by years of immersion in Japanese traditions and principles, I share these insights not as a distant observer but as someone profoundly transformed by their essence. From the philosophy of Ikigai, which illuminates the path to purpose, to the mindful practice of Hara hachi bu, which teaches us the art of moderation, each concept has the power to shift our perspective and enrich our lives.

As you embark on this journey, I encourage you to approach it with an open mind and a willing heart. The principles within these pages are not bound by geography or culture; they are universal truths that transcend borders and resonate with the soul.

Let this book serve as your companion in discovering not only the beauty of Japanese wisdom but also the untapped potential within yourself. Together, let us embark on a journey of transformation—one step, one moment, and one principle at a time.

DEDICATION

To my Mother and Father, the pillars of my character. From you, I learned the essence of hard work, honesty, and humbleness. My mother, with her unwavering patience, and my father, with his steadfast honesty, shaped the core values that guide me through life.

To my Grandfather (Nana), whose graceful persona left a lasting impression on how to carry oneself with dignity and respect. To my Grandmother (Nani), whose quiet wisdom and nurturing spirit instilled in me the importance of compassion and resilience.

To my wife, Pooja, whose relentless encouragement and belief in me taught me the power of perseverance. You pushed me beyond my limits, showing me that nothing is impossible and that everyone has something extraordinary within them.

To my elder Sister, who showed me the importance of kindness in every situation, no matter how challenging.

To my elder Brother, who has been a constant source of strength and support, teaching me the value of resilience and determination.

And to all my Family members, whose love and guidance have been the foundation of my journey. Your support has been my greatest asset.

To all my Friends, who have stood by me through thick and thin, thank you for being an integral part of my journey.

This book is a testament to the values and lessons you have all imparted to me.

ACKNOWLEDGEMENT

I am deeply grateful to my friend Lovekush, whose guidance throughout this writing journey has been invaluable. Your insights and support have shaped this book in more ways than I can express.

A heartfelt thank you to Ashvirya, who has been instrumental in helping me refine and improve this work in every aspect. Your contributions have made this book better than I could have imagined.

I also want to extend my deepest appreciation to my Japanese friends and mentors, who have been my windows into the rich and profound Japanese culture. Kazumi Tanaka, Aki Hozumi, Chirantan Pawel, Manoranjan Singh, Abhishek Singh, and many others—thank you for sharing your knowledge and experiences with me. Your influence is woven into every chapter of this book.

This work is a reflection of all the wisdom and support I have received from each of you. Thank you for being an integral part of this journey.

TABLE OF CONTENT

INTRODUCTION

The Path to a Fulfilled Life through Japanese Principles

In a world that often feels chaotic and overwhelming, the pursuit of a balanced, meaningful life has never been more essential. We are constantly bombarded with messages that equate success with material wealth, relentless productivity, and the pursuit of perfection. Yet, these ideals often leave us feeling exhausted, unfulfilled, and disconnected from what truly matters.

This book offers an alternative path—one inspired by timeless Japanese principles that have guided generations in leading lives of purpose, simplicity, and contentment. Drawing from my own experiences living and working in Japan, I've come to appreciate the profound wisdom embedded in Japanese culture. These principles have not only shaped my personal and professional life but have also provided me with tools to navigate life's challenges with grace and resilience.

In these pages, you'll discover six key Japanese concepts that can transform your life:

Ikigai: Discovering Your Purpose – Learn how to find your true calling by aligning what you love, what you're good at, what the world needs, and what you can be paid for.

Kaizen: Continuous Improvement – Embrace the power of small, steady steps to achieve lasting personal and professional growth.

The Pomodoro Technique: Enhancing Productivity – Master your time and boost your productivity using this simple yet effective time management method.

Hara hachi-bu: The Art of Moderation – Adopt the Japanese practice of mindful eating and moderation to improve your health and well-being.

Embracing Minimalism: The Japanese Art of Decluttering – Simplify your life by letting go of excess and focusing on what truly adds value.

Wabi-Sabi: Embracing Imperfection – Find beauty in the imperfect and incomplete, and cultivate a sense of peace by accepting life's inevitable imperfections.

Each chapter delves into one of these principles, offering practical advice, real-life examples, and actionable steps to integrate these timeless concepts into your daily routine. Whether you are looking to improve your personal life, advance in your career, or simply find more joy and meaning in your everyday activities, these Japanese principles provide a roadmap to a more fulfilled and harmonious life.

As you embark on this journey, remember that transformation doesn't happen overnight. Just as the Japanese bamboo grows strong and resilient over time, so too will you grow by embracing these principles with patience and persistence. Together, let's explore how the wisdom of Japan can help you create a life of balance, purpose, and true happiness.

CHAPTER 1 DISCOVERING IKIGAI

Discovering Ikigai – The Journey to Finding Your Purpose

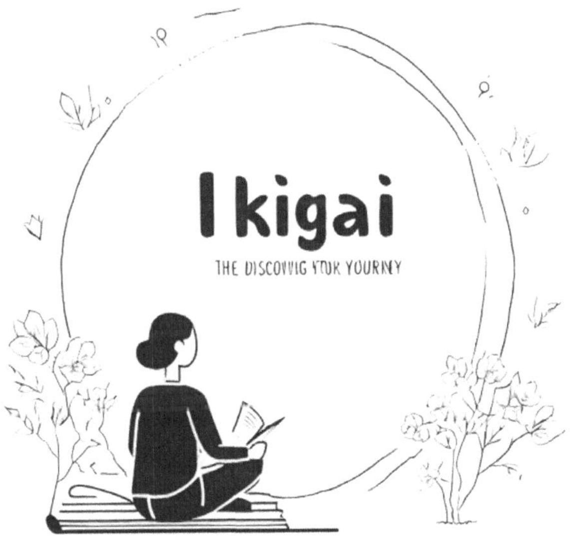

Introduction: A Life of Purpose

Imagine waking up each day with a profound sense of purpose, knowing exactly what drives you and why you do what you do. This is not just a dream but a reality that many strive for and achieve through the concept of Ikigai. In Japan, Ikigai represents the intersection of what you love, what you're good at, what the world needs, and what you can be compensated for. It's a blend of passion, mission, vocation, and profession, creating a harmonious balance that leads to a fulfilling life.

The power of Ikigai is not just a theoretical idea but is supported by practical evidence. For instance, the residents of Okinawa, Japan, are known for their exceptional longevity and well-being, which many attribute to their strong sense of Ikigai. A study conducted by the National Geographic Society and the National Institute on Aging found that Okinawans, who often have a clear sense of purpose, enjoy lower rates of chronic diseases and have some of the highest life expectancies in the world. Their daily routines, which are deeply embedded with meaningful activities, demonstrate how living with a clear purpose can have tangible benefits on one's health and happiness.

Ikigai is more than just a concept; it's a way of life that can bring profound satisfaction and health benefits. By finding and living your Ikigai, you can achieve a balanced and fulfilling life, waking up each day with a clear sense of purpose and direction.

The Essence of Ikigai

Ikigai, translating to "reason for being," is more than just a life philosophy. It's a profound guide to understanding oneself deeply and living a meaningful life. Imagine waking up each day with a sense of enthusiasm and purpose, knowing that what you do aligns perfectly with who you are. This is the essence of Ikigai. It's about discovering the delicate balance where your passions, talents, societal contributions, and financial needs intersect. This balance, or sweet spot, is where you find true fulfillment and contentment.

Finding your Ikigai involves a journey of introspection and self-discovery. It requires you to look inward and ask yourself fundamental questions about what truly excites you and brings you joy. Think about the activities that make you lose track of time, the skills you have honed over the years, and the unique talents that set you apart. This is not just about identifying your hobbies or interests, but about understanding what fuels your inner drive and makes you feel alive.

Next, it's essential to recognize your skills and strengths. What are you exceptionally good at? What do others often seek your help with? This step is about acknowledging your capabilities and understanding how you can use them to make a positive impact. Your skills are the tools that will help you achieve your Ikigai.

Ikigai also involves looking beyond yourself to see how you can contribute to society. What problems are you passionate about solving? What needs do you see in your community or the world at large? This perspective shifts the focus from personal gain to collective benefit, emphasizing the importance of making a difference and leaving a positive mark on the world. It's about finding ways to serve others, whether through your work, volunteer activities, or personal projects.

Lastly, financial sustainability is a crucial component of Ikigai. While passion and purpose are vital, they must be balanced with practical considerations. This means finding ways to monetize your passions and skills, ensuring that you can support yourself and your loved ones. It's about creating a livelihood that aligns with your values and allows you to live comfortably while pursuing your purpose.

The equilibrium achieved through Ikigai brings immense personal satisfaction. It fosters a sense of harmony between your inner desires and external actions, leading to a life that feels authentic and fulfilling. But the benefits of Ikigai extend beyond personal happiness. Research has shown that having a clear sense of purpose can positively impact your health. Studies, such as those conducted by Tohoku University, have found that individuals with a defined Ikigai experience lower stress levels, better mental health, and reduced risks of cardiovascular diseases. This sense of purpose can even contribute to a longer life, as it motivates healthier lifestyle choices and fosters resilience against life's challenges.

Take, for example, the story of Mrs. Yamada, lives near Kirigaoka, a woman in her late sixties who found her Ikigai in gardening. After retiring from a corporate job, she started a small community garden in her neighborhood. Gardening was something she loved and was skilled at, and it allowed her to connect with her community by providing fresh produce and a beautiful green space. She also sold some of her produce at local markets, ensuring a modest but steady income. Mrs. Yamada's garden became her Ikigai – a perfect blend of passion, skill, societal contribution, and financial sustainability. It brought her immense joy and satisfaction, and she often shared how it made her feel healthier and more energetic than ever before.

In essence, Ikigai is about finding that unique intersection where what you love, what you are good at, what the world needs, and what you can be paid for converge. It's a journey that requires patience, reflection, and a willingness to explore new possibilities. But once found, your Ikigai becomes a powerful source of motivation and fulfillment, guiding you towards a life of purpose, health, and happiness. By embracing this concept, you open the door to a deeper understanding of yourself and a richer, more meaningful life.

The Science Behind Ikigai

Studies have shown that having a sense of purpose is linked to various health benefits. One notable research conducted by Tohoku University delves into the profound impacts of Ikigai on health and longevity. This extensive study, which involved over 43,000 Japanese adults, revealed that individuals who identified and embraced their Ikigai had significantly lower risks of cardiovascular diseases and exhibited longer life expectancy.

The study highlighted several mechanisms through which Ikigai contributes to better health. Firstly, a clear sense of purpose can act as a powerful stress reducer. People with a defined Ikigai tend to experience lower levels of stress and anxiety, which are well-known contributors to various health issues, including heart disease. By having a guiding purpose, individuals are better equipped to cope with life's challenges, reducing the harmful effects of stress on the body.

Moreover, the study found that people with Ikigai generally lead healthier lifestyles. They are more likely to engage in regular physical activity, maintain a balanced diet, and avoid harmful habits like smoking and excessive drinking. This is because a sense of purpose often drives individuals to take better care of themselves to fulfill their goals and responsibilities. For example, someone whose Ikigai involves taking care of their grandchildren will be motivated to stay healthy and active to continue being there for their loved ones.

The mental health benefits of Ikigai are also significant. The study showed that individuals with a strong sense of purpose experience higher levels of overall happiness and life satisfaction. They are less prone to depression and anxiety, which can have cascading positive effects on their physical health. Mental well-being is closely tied to physical health, and by fostering a positive mental state, Ikigai contributes to overall better health outcomes.

Additionally, the research indicated that having Ikigai encourages social engagement and community involvement. People with a clear purpose are often more socially active, which has been linked to better health and longevity. Social connections provide emotional support, reduce feelings of loneliness, and promote a sense of belonging, all of which are crucial for maintaining good health.

To illustrate, let's consider a practical example from the study. One participant, Mrs. Yamamoto, a retired teacher, found her Ikigai while volunteering at a local school. Her daily interactions with children and the fulfillment she gained from contributing to their education kept her physically active and mentally sharp. She reported lower stress levels, better physical health, and an overall sense of happiness and contentment. Mrs. Yamamoto's experience underscores how Ikigai can lead to a healthier and more fulfilling life.

In summary, the Tohoku University study provides compelling evidence that identifying and living your Ikigai can lead to numerous health benefits. By reducing stress, promoting healthier lifestyles, enhancing mental well-being, and encouraging social connections, Ikigai serves as a powerful tool for achieving better health and longevity. This research highlights the transformative potential of finding and embracing your purpose, reinforcing the importance of Ikigai in achieving a balanced and fulfilling life.

Reflecting on Your Passions

Discovering your Ikigai begins with deep introspection. It's a journey inward, where you examine what truly excites you and brings you joy. Start by asking yourself some fundamental questions: What activities make you lose track of time? What hobbies or tasks do you find yourself eagerly looking forward to? These reflections help uncover your genuine passions and interests, which form the foundation of your Ikigai.

Consider making a list of activities that you love doing. These could range from creative pursuits like painting or writing to more dynamic activities like hiking or playing sports. Think about moments when you felt completely immersed and content. For instance, maybe you lose yourself in the flow of writing stories, or perhaps you find joy in helping others through volunteer work. Reflecting on these experiences can provide valuable insights into your true passions.

To illustrate, let's look at the story of Kenji, a middle-aged office worker. Kenji spent years in a corporate job that paid well but left him feeling unfulfilled. During a period of self-reflection, he remembered how much he enjoyed gardening as a child. He decided to rekindle this passion by starting a small vegetable garden in his backyard. This activity brought him immense joy and a sense of peace. Eventually, Kenji expanded his garden and began sharing his produce with neighbors, which added a new layer of satisfaction and community involvement to his life. Through this process, Kenji discovered that his passion for gardening was a key component of his Ikigai.

Another practical approach is to keep a journal. Document your daily activities and note how each one makes you feel. Pay attention to the tasks that energize you versus those that drain you. Over time, patterns will emerge, highlighting your true passions. For example, if you find that you consistently feel excited and motivated when cooking new recipes, this could be a significant clue to your Ikigai.

Additionally, talking to friends, family, and colleagues can provide valuable feedback. Often, those close to you can see your passions more clearly than you can. They might notice that you light up when discussing certain topics or activities. Engaging in conversations about what you enjoy can help you gain a clearer perspective on your passions.

Exploring new activities can also be revealing. Sometimes, you may not fully know what excites you until you try something new. Take classes, join clubs, or volunteer in different areas to expose yourself to a variety of experiences. For instance, if you've always been curious about pottery, sign up for a workshop. You might discover a newfound passion that you had never considered before.

Reflecting on your passions is a crucial first step in finding your Ikigai. It's about identifying what you love and what makes you feel truly alive. By engaging in introspection, journaling, seeking feedback, and exploring new activities, you can uncover the interests and activities that are central to your sense of purpose. This foundation will guide you towards a more fulfilling and meaningful life.

Recognizing Your Skills

The next step in discovering your Ikigai is to acknowledge your strengths and skills. This involves taking a close look at what you excel at and considering how you can leverage these abilities in your daily life. Your skills might include talents you've developed over time, such as through education or work experience, or they might be innate abilities that you naturally possess.

Begin by making a list of your skills. Reflect on your professional and personal life to identify areas where you consistently perform well. Think about the tasks that come easily to you or the activities where others frequently seek your assistance. These are often indicators of your strengths. For instance, if you're always the go-to person for organizing events or solving technical problems, these might be key skills to consider.

To make this process more concrete, let's consider the story of Hana, a graphic designer. Hana had always been artistically inclined, even from a young age. Her skill in visual arts led her to pursue a career in graphic design, where she excelled in creating compelling visuals and branding materials. However, she felt something was missing in her work. Through introspection, Hana realized that while she was good at graphic design, she also had a passion for teaching and mentoring others. She decided to combine these skills by starting a design workshop for aspiring artists. This new venture allowed her to leverage her artistic skills while fulfilling her desire to help others, ultimately leading her to her Ikigai.

Another practical approach to recognizing your skills is to seek feedback from others. Sometimes, it's difficult to see our own strengths objectively. Ask colleagues, friends, and family members what they believe you excel at. Their insights can provide a more rounded view of your abilities. For example, you might think of yourself as just good at numbers, but others might see you as a natural problem-solver and strategist.

You can also take various skill assessments and personality tests. Tools like the StrengthsFinder, Myers-Briggs Type Indicator (MBTI), or the VIA Character Strengths Survey can help identify your core competencies and natural inclinations. These assessments can provide a structured way to understand your strengths and how you can use them effectively.

Consider the story of Aki, a manager in a logistics company. Aki was known for her excellent organizational skills and ability to keep her team motivated and on track. She took a leadership assessment and discovered that her strengths lay in strategic thinking and people management. With this knowledge, Aki started mentoring other managers and eventually transitioned into a role where she focused on leadership development within her organization. By recognizing and embracing her skills, Aki found greater fulfillment and purpose in her career.

Recognizing your skills also means understanding how they can be applied in different contexts. Skills are often transferable, meaning they can be used in various settings. For example, if you are good at public speaking, this skill can be valuable in numerous areas, from teaching and sales to community leadership and advocacy. Think broadly about how your abilities can be utilized in different scenarios.

Moreover, don't overlook the importance of soft skills, such as communication, empathy, and teamwork. These interpersonal skills are often just as critical as technical abilities. For instance, if you have a knack for understanding and connecting with people, this could be a significant component of your Ikigai, especially in roles that involve customer service, counseling, or team management.

Recognizing your skills is about more than just identifying what you are good at; it's about understanding how these abilities can contribute to your overall sense of purpose and fulfillment. By acknowledging your strengths and finding ways to apply them in meaningful ways, you move closer to discovering your Ikigai. This step is crucial in aligning your daily activities with your innate talents, ultimately leading to a more satisfying and purposeful life.

Identifying Societal Needs

Ikigai also involves recognizing what the world needs. This step encourages you to think beyond personal interests and skills to consider how you can contribute to society. By identifying the problems you are passionate about solving or the needs you see in your community or the broader society, you ensure that your purpose aligns with a greater good, providing a sense of contribution and fulfillment.

Start by reflecting on the issues that resonate with you on a personal level. These could be social, environmental, or economic problems that you feel strongly about. Consider the causes that stir your emotions and make you want to take action. For example, you might feel a deep concern for environmental conservation, social justice, education, or public health. Identifying these passions can guide you toward areas where your efforts can make a meaningful impact.

Take the story of Naoko, a nurse who always felt a strong compassion for the elderly. While she loved her job, she felt that her work could have a broader impact. During her community outreach, she noticed a significant number of elderly people living in isolation, struggling with loneliness and mental health issues. This observation sparked an idea. Naoko started a volunteer program where she and other nurses visited elderly residents, providing not only medical care but also companionship and social interaction. By addressing this societal need, Naoko found a deeper sense of fulfillment in her work, aligning her professional skills with a meaningful cause.

Another approach to identifying societal needs is to engage with your community. Attend local meetings, volunteer with different organizations, and talk to people from various backgrounds. These interactions can provide insights into the challenges and needs of your community. For instance, you might discover that there is a shortage of educational resources in your neighborhood schools or that there are many homeless individuals in need of support. Understanding these needs can help you identify where your skills and passions can be most effectively utilized.

Consider the story of Hiroshi, an engineer who was passionate about renewable energy. He realized that many rural communities in Japan lacked access to reliable electricity, hindering their development. Hiroshi decided to use his engineering skills to develop affordable solar power solutions for these areas. By addressing this critical need, he not only improved the quality of life for many people but also found a profound sense of purpose in his work.

Additionally, stay informed about global issues. Read news articles, watch documentaries, and follow organizations that work on causes you care about. This can broaden your perspective and help you see where your contributions could make a significant difference. For example, if you are passionate about education, learning about global literacy rates and educational disparities can inspire you to take action, whether through teaching, fundraising, or advocacy.

Sometimes, identifying societal needs involves looking at the broader impact of your current work. Ask yourself how your profession or business can contribute positively to society. For instance, if you run a business, consider how you can implement sustainable practices, support local communities, or create products that solve real-world problems. This approach not only benefits society but can also enhance your business's reputation and success.

Take the example of Keiko, a successful restaurateur. She noticed the increasing issue of food waste in the hospitality industry and decided to address it by implementing a zero-waste policy in her restaurants. She partnered with local farmers to use surplus produce, composted food scraps, and donated excess food to shelters. Keiko's efforts not only reduced waste but also raised awareness about sustainability, aligning her business practices with a greater societal need.

Identifying societal needs is a crucial step in discovering your Ikigai. It ensures that your purpose is not just self-serving but also contributes to the well-being of others. By focusing on the problems you are passionate about solving and the needs you see in your community or the broader society, you create a sense of contribution and fulfillment that goes beyond personal satisfaction. This alignment with a greater good enriches your life and makes your pursuits more meaningful, helping you achieve a truly fulfilling and purposeful existence.

Evaluating Potential Earnings

The final step in discovering your Ikigai is to consider what you can be paid for. This aspect ties your passions and skills to a sustainable livelihood, ensuring that your pursuit of purpose is financially viable. It's about finding ways to monetize your interests and talents so that you can continue doing what you love while also supporting yourself and your family.

Begin by assessing your current financial needs and goals. Think about your lifestyle, expenses, and any financial obligations you have. This will give you a clear picture of what you need to earn to maintain your standard of living. Next, explore the various ways you can monetize your skills and passions. This might involve looking at your current job or career path and seeing how it aligns with your Ikigai or considering new opportunities that better match your interests and abilities.

Let’s consider the story of Yuki, a talented baker who always loved creating intricate and delicious pastries. While she enjoyed baking as a hobby, she initially struggled to see how it could support her financially. After some research and reflection, Yuki decided to start a small bakery, combining her passion for baking with her entrepreneurial skills. She began by selling her pastries at local farmers' markets and through online orders. Over time, her business grew, allowing her to open a physical bakery. Yuki’s story illustrates how identifying a viable market for her skills enabled her to turn her passion into a successful and sustainable career.

Another approach is to look for roles or industries that value your unique combination of skills and passions. For example, if you are passionate about writing and have a knack for storytelling, you might explore careers in journalism, content creation, or publishing. If you enjoy teaching and have expertise in a particular subject, consider roles in education or training. It’s about finding the intersection where your interests meet market demand.

Consider the example of Takeshi, a software engineer with a passion for education. While he enjoyed his work in tech, he felt a calling to help others learn and grow in the field. Takeshi started creating online coding courses and tutoring students in his spare time. Eventually, he was able to transition into a full-time role as an online educator, leveraging his technical skills and passion for teaching to create a financially sustainable career. This move not only provided Takeshi with a steady income but also allowed him to fulfill his Ikigai by making a positive impact on others.

Additionally, think about how you can diversify your income streams. Relying on a single source of income can be risky, so consider how you can use your skills in multiple ways. For instance, you might work a full-time job while pursuing freelance projects, consulting, or starting a side business. This approach not only increases your earning potential but also provides more opportunities to align your work with your Ikigai.

For instance, consider Hiro, an artist who worked in a corporate graphic design job. While the job paid well, Hiro felt creatively stifled. To diversify his income, he started selling his own artwork online and taking freelance commissions. This not only provided additional income but also allowed Hiro to express his creativity and build a reputation as an independent artist. Over time, his freelance work grew to a point where he could leave his corporate job and focus entirely on his art. By finding multiple ways to monetize his skills, Hiro was able to create a financially viable path that aligned with his true passions.

Networking and professional development are also key. Building a strong professional network can open up new opportunities and help you stay informed about trends in your field. Attend industry events, join professional associations, and connect with mentors who can provide guidance and support. Continuous learning and skill development can also enhance your marketability, ensuring that you remain competitive and can command a fair wage for your talents.

Consider the story of Aiko, a fashion designer who wanted to break into the sustainable fashion industry. By attending industry conferences, participating in workshops, and connecting with other professionals, Aiko gained valuable insights and contacts that helped her launch her own eco-friendly fashion line. Her commitment to continuous learning and networking enabled her to turn her passion into a successful and financially rewarding business.

Evaluating potential earnings is a crucial step in discovering your Ikigai. It ensures that your pursuit of purpose is not only fulfilling but also financially sustainable. By identifying viable ways to monetize your skills and passions, exploring diverse income streams, and investing in professional development, you can create a career that supports both your personal and financial goals. This balance is essential for long-term success and happiness, allowing you to live a life that is both meaningful and sustainable.

Personal Experience: Ikigai in Action

When I first traveled to Japan, I was struck by the dedication and vigor of the elderly population. Unlike many other countries where people over 60 or 70 often retire and enjoy a more sedentary lifestyle, Japanese seniors remain remarkably active. I observed many elderly individuals engaging in physical labor and community service. Even those who did not have formal jobs took it upon themselves to keep the streets clean, using long forks to pick up litter voluntarily. This kind of work, often considered menial in other cultures, was carried out with pride and a sense of purpose. Many were also involved in roles like housekeeping, displaying a willingness to stay active and contribute meaningfully to society. This widespread practice among Japan's elderly is a testament to the country's embrace of

Ikigai, illustrating how a clear sense of purpose can lead to a more active and fulfilling life.

A Deeper Dive into Ikigai

To better understand the concept of Ikigai, it helps to look at specific examples and stories from Japan. One notable example is the community of Ogimi, a village in Okinawa known for its high population of centenarians. Residents of Ogimi often attribute their longevity to having a clear sense of purpose in life, or Ikigai. Many continue to work in their gardens, participate in community activities, and take care of their families well into their 90s and beyond. Their daily routines are filled with meaningful activities that give them a sense of accomplishment and connection.

Another inspiring story is that of Jiro Ono, the world-renowned sushi chef who continues to perfect his craft well into his 90s. Jiro's dedication to sushi is a perfect example of Ikigai. He wakes up every day with the goal of making the best sushi possible, constantly refining his techniques and mentoring younger chefs. His work is not just a job but a lifelong pursuit that brings him joy and fulfillment. Jiro's story demonstrates how deeply intertwined professional dedication and personal passion can create a lasting sense of purpose.

The Role of Community and Social Connections

The concept of Ikigai is also deeply rooted in social connections and community involvement. In Japan, there is a strong emphasis on maintaining relationships and contributing to the community. This is evident in the numerous festivals, volunteer activities, and community gatherings that take place regularly. People of all ages come together to celebrate, work, and support one another, creating a strong sense of belonging and purpose.

Take the example of Mrs. Tanaka, a retired schoolteacher who lives in Tokyo. After retiring, she could have chosen a quiet life at home, but instead, she became actively involved in her local community center. She started a book club, volunteers at the library, and helps organize events for local children. Mrs. Tanaka finds joy in sharing her love of reading and education with others, and her activities provide her with a sense of purpose and connection. Her story highlights how staying engaged with the community can enrich one's life and contribute to overall well-being.

Ikigai in the Workplace

Incorporating Ikigai into the workplace is another area where the Japanese excel. Companies often encourage employees to find meaning in their work and align their personal values with the company's mission. This approach not only enhances job satisfaction but also boosts productivity and innovation.

For instance, at Toyota, the philosophy of continuous improvement, or Kaizen, is a key component of the company's success. Employees at all levels are encouraged to suggest improvements and take ownership of their work. This sense of involvement and contribution helps employees find their Ikigai within their roles, leading to a more motivated and engaged workforce. Similarly, at companies like Uniqlo, employees are trained to see their work as part of a larger mission to provide high-quality, affordable clothing to people around the world, which helps them find meaning and satisfaction in their jobs.

The Impact of Ikigai on Health and Longevity

The link between Ikigai and health is well-documented. Research conducted by Tohoku University found that individuals with a clear sense of purpose tend to have lower risks of cardiovascular diseases and generally live longer. This is because having a sense of purpose can reduce stress, improve mental health, and promote healthier lifestyles.

Consider the story of Kenji, a retired engineer who found his Ikigai in painting. After retiring, Kenji felt lost without the structure and purpose that his job provided. He decided to pursue his long-forgotten passion for painting. Kenji started taking art classes and eventually began teaching painting to others. This new sense of purpose not only gave him a reason to wake up each morning but also led to improved health and well-being. He became more active, engaged with a new community of artists, and found immense joy in his daily life.

Embracing Ikigai in Daily Life

Embracing Ikigai in daily life involves making intentional choices that align with your passions, skills, and the needs of the world around you. It's about finding balance and making time for activities that bring you joy and fulfillment.

For example, Akiko, a young mother and graphic designer, found her Ikigai in combining her love for design with her passion for sustainable living. She started creating eco-friendly children's books that educate kids about the environment. This project not only utilizes her design skills but also addresses a societal need and aligns with her personal values. Akiko's story shows how finding your Ikigai can lead to a more meaningful and fulfilling life.

Conclusion

The concept of Ikigai offers profound insights into living a purposeful and fulfilling life. It encourages us to reflect on our passions, recognize our skills, identify societal needs, and evaluate potential earnings. By aligning these elements, we can find a sense of purpose that brings joy, satisfaction, and meaning to our lives.

Whether through personal hobbies, professional endeavors, or community involvement, Ikigai teaches us that a life of purpose is not only possible but also essential for our overall well-being. The stories of the elderly in Japan, the communities in Okinawa, and individuals like Jiro Ono, Mrs. Uchida, and Kenji illustrate the transformative power of Ikigai. By embracing this concept, we can create lives that are not only successful but also deeply fulfilling and enriching.

CHAPTER 2 KAIZEN

Kaizen - Continuous Improvement

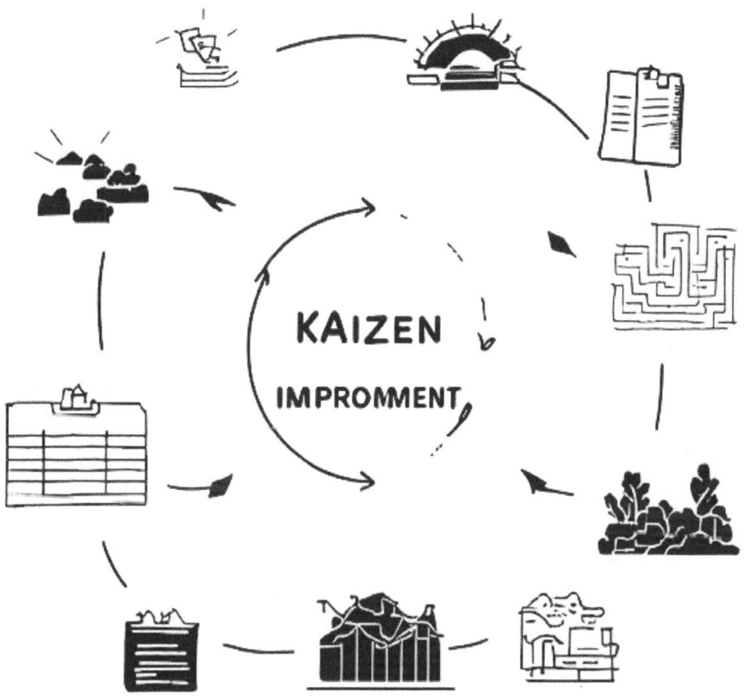

Introduction: The Power of Small Steps

In our quest for personal growth and professional excellence, it's common to desire immediate and dramatic transformations. We often find ourselves setting ambitious goals and expecting swift, sweeping changes. However, the Japanese philosophy of Kaizen offers a different approach, one that emphasizes the power of small, steady steps. Kaizen, meaning "continuous improvement," teaches that sustainable progress and lasting improvement stem from the gradual accumulation of minor, consistent changes over time.

This principle is not merely theoretical; it is deeply rooted in Japanese culture and business practices. Kaizen has been instrumental in shaping the success of numerous Japanese enterprises, most notably in the manufacturing sector. The philosophy encourages a mindset of constant, incremental enhancement, which stands in stark contrast to the Western tendency to seek quick fixes and large-scale overhauls.

Understanding Kaizen involves appreciating its simplicity and practicality. By focusing on making small, manageable changes, we reduce the risk of burnout and maintain a steady trajectory toward our goals. This approach fosters a culture of continuous improvement, where every minor adjustment contributes to a larger, more significant transformation.

The essence of Kaizen lies in its application to everyday life. Whether it's personal habits, professional skills, or organizational processes, the principle of continuous improvement can be applied universally. By breaking down daunting tasks into smaller, achievable steps, we make progress more attainable and less overwhelming. This method not only enhances productivity but also cultivates a sense of accomplishment and motivation.

In this chapter, we will explore the core tenets of Kaizen and its profound impact on various aspects of life. Through real-life examples and practical applications, we will see how the philosophy of Kaizen can lead to remarkable improvements. From personal anecdotes to corporate success stories, the power of small steps will become evident, demonstrating that true and lasting change is within our reach, one small step at a time.

The Origins of Kaizen

The concept of Kaizen gained prominence in Japan during the post-World War II era, particularly in the manufacturing industry. After the war, Japan's economy was in dire need of revitalization. With the assistance of American management consultants like W. Edwards Deming, Japanese industries began to adopt new methodologies to improve efficiency and quality. Among these methodologies, Kaizen emerged as a cornerstone, emphasizing the importance of small, continuous improvements in processes, products, and services.

Toyota, one of Japan's most successful companies, is a prime example of Kaizen in action. The Toyota Production System, often considered the epitome of Kaizen, focuses on eliminating waste, improving efficiency, and enhancing quality through small, consistent changes. Employees at all levels are encouraged to suggest improvements, fostering a culture of continuous enhancement and innovation.

Embracing Kaizen: A Journey of Incremental Progress

To truly understand the transformative power of Kaizen, consider the analogy of climbing a mountain. Imagine standing at the base, gazing up at the daunting peak. The journey to the top seems overwhelming, perhaps even impossible. However, if you focus on taking one step at a time, the climb becomes manageable. Each small step brings you closer to the summit, and before long, you find yourself making steady progress.

This is the essence of Kaizen. Instead of being paralyzed by the enormity of a goal, break it down into smaller, actionable steps. For instance, if your aim is to write a book, start by dedicating just 15 minutes a day to writing. Over time, these short, consistent writing sessions will accumulate, leading to substantial progress.

The Ripple Effect of Small Changes

The power of Kaizen lies in its ripple effect. One small change can set off a chain reaction, leading to broader improvements. For example, deciding to wake up 10 minutes earlier each day might initially seem insignificant. However, this small adjustment can lead to a series of positive changes: a more relaxed morning routine, a healthy breakfast, and a more focused start to the day. These improvements can then enhance your overall productivity and well-being.

This principle applies not only to individuals but also to organizations. In a corporate setting, encouraging employees to suggest small improvements in their workflow can lead to significant enhancements in efficiency and morale. When everyone is committed to continuous improvement, the cumulative effect can be transformative.

The Kaizen Mindset: Patience and Persistence

One of the key elements of Kaizen is cultivating a mindset of patience and persistence. Small steps may not yield immediate, dramatic results, but their cumulative impact over time can be profound. This requires a shift in perspective, recognizing that lasting change is a marathon, not a sprint.

Adopting a Kaizen mindset means embracing the journey of improvement with an open and proactive attitude. It involves being willing to experiment with small changes, learning from each step, and continuously seeking opportunities for enhancement. This approach fosters resilience and adaptability, essential qualities for navigating the complexities of personal and professional life.

Practical Applications of Kaizen

Kaizen's principles can be applied in various areas of life, from personal habits to professional development. Here are some practical ways to incorporate Kaizen into your daily routine:

Personal Development:

Break down your goals into smaller, actionable steps. For example, if you want to improve your fitness, start with a

10-minute daily workout and gradually increase the duration and intensity.

Implement small changes in your daily routine, such as decluttering one room at a time or dedicating a few minutes each day to reading or meditation.

Professional Growth:

Identify areas for improvement in your work processes. This could involve optimizing your email management, streamlining your project workflows, or enhancing your time management skills.

Encourage a culture of continuous improvement in your workplace by soliciting feedback and suggestions from colleagues and team members.

Health and Well-being:

Focus on small, sustainable changes to your diet and exercise habits. For instance, gradually reduce your sugar intake or incorporate more fruits and vegetables into your meals.

Practice mindfulness and stress reduction techniques, such as deep breathing exercises or short meditation sessions, to enhance your mental well-being.

Kaizen in Daily Life

While Kaizen originated in the industrial sector, its principles are equally applicable to personal development and daily life. The philosophy encourages us to break down large, daunting tasks into smaller, manageable steps, making it easier to achieve our goals without feeling overwhelmed.

Personal Experience: Embracing Kaizen in My Life

When I first encountered the concept of Kaizen during a visit to Japan, I was immediately intrigued by its simplicity and effectiveness. The meticulous dedication of Japanese workers, who continually seek to improve even the smallest aspects of their tasks, was inspiring. Determined to incorporate Kaizen into my own life, I started with small, manageable changes.

I began by integrating small efforts into my daily routine. Before leaving for Japan, over the span of five years, I managed to accomplish significant milestones: I learned new technologies, completed my Master's degree, and even wrote my first book. Initially, these goals seemed daunting, but by breaking them down into smaller, achievable tasks, I made steady progress. For instance, I dedicated a few minutes each day to studying new tech trends, which eventually led to a comprehensive understanding and proficiency in those technologies. Similarly, I allocated specific times for my academic work and writing, ensuring consistent progress without feeling overwhelmed.

Next, I applied Kaizen to my home organization. Instead of attempting a massive decluttering project, I focused on organizing one drawer at a time. This approach made the task less overwhelming and more manageable. Over several weeks, my living space became significantly more organized, and the sense of order brought a noticeable calm to my daily life.

One particularly impactful experience involved explaining the Kaizen philosophy to a non-Japanese colleague. I shared the idea that even a 0.1% improvement each day could lead to remarkable results over time. Initially skeptical, my colleague decided to give it a try, applying small daily improvements to his work processes. Over the following months, he was amazed by the cumulative effect of these minor adjustments. His productivity increased, and he found new motivation in his work, illustrating the transformative power of Kaizen.

This same colleague applied Kaizen to his fitness routine. Rather than setting an ambitious goal of intense workouts right away, he started with short, manageable exercises. Initially, he committed to just a few minutes of physical activity each day, gradually increasing the duration and intensity. This incremental approach helped him build a sustainable exercise habit without the risk of burnout or injury. Today, he is the fittest person in the whole office, a testament to the effectiveness of Kaizen in achieving long-term fitness goals.

These small, incremental changes had a profound impact on my life. Over time, I noticed significant improvements in my productivity, organization, and overall well-being. The key to Kaizen is consistency. By committing to small daily improvements, I was able to achieve my larger goals without feeling overwhelmed.

Incorporating Kaizen into my life taught me the value of patience and persistence. Each small step forward, no matter how minor, contributed to a larger journey of continuous improvement. This philosophy helped me appreciate the process of growth and development, rather than focusing solely on the end results.

The Science Behind Kaizen

The efficacy of Kaizen in fostering long-term improvement is well-supported by scientific research. A notable study conducted at the University of California investigated how incremental changes impact lifestyle adjustments and found compelling evidence in favor of the Kaizen approach. This research highlighted that small, consistent modifications are often more effective and sustainable compared to large, abrupt changes. The study demonstrated that gradual adjustments reduce the risk of burnout, as they allow individuals to adapt to changes at a manageable pace. This steady progression helps maintain motivation and enhances the likelihood of achieving lasting results.

Additionally, Kaizen promotes the development of a growth mindset, a concept extensively studied in psychology. By encouraging individuals to view challenges as opportunities for growth rather than insurmountable barriers, Kaizen helps foster resilience and adaptability. Research in this area underscores the importance of adopting a proactive approach to problem-solving, where challenges are seen as chances for improvement rather than failures. This mindset shift is crucial for both personal and professional development, as it supports continuous learning and encourages a constructive response to setbacks.

The research also suggests that the Kaizen approach aligns with the principles of behavioral science, which emphasize the power of small, manageable steps in achieving significant changes. By breaking down larger goals into smaller, actionable tasks, Kaizen makes progress more attainable and less overwhelming. This strategy not only facilitates steady improvement but also enhances overall well-being by promoting a sense of accomplishment and forward momentum.

In essence, the scientific backing for Kaizen underscores its effectiveness as a method for achieving meaningful and sustainable improvement. By leveraging the power of incremental changes and fostering a growth-oriented mindset, individuals can make significant strides in their personal and professional lives.

Practical Applications of Kaizen

Setting Goals with Kaizen

Applying Kaizen begins with setting precise, achievable goals. The key is to decompose these goals into smaller, actionable steps that can be accomplished on a regular basis. For instance, if your goal is to enhance your physical fitness, you could initiate the process with brief daily exercise sessions. These can start as short as five minutes and gradually extend in duration and intensity as your endurance builds. This incremental approach helps in creating a sustainable fitness routine without overwhelming you. Additionally, acknowledging and celebrating these minor achievements—such as completing a workout session—keeps you motivated and reinforces your commitment to your fitness journey.

Creating a Kaizen Board

A Kaizen board serves as a practical tool for tracking progress and managing improvements visually. To set up a Kaizen board, divide it into three distinct sections: "To Do," "In Progress," and "Completed." Use sticky notes to represent each task or improvement you intend to undertake, moving these notes across the board as you progress. This visual aid not only provides a clear overview of your tasks but also helps in maintaining motivation. Seeing tasks shift from "To Do" to "Completed" can offer a tangible sense of accomplishment and drive continued effort.

The Five Whys Technique

The Five Whys technique is a problem-solving tool used in Kaizen to identify the root causes of issues. By asking "why" repeatedly—typically five times—you can dig deeper into the underlying causes of a problem. For example, if you're facing challenges with time management, you might begin by asking:

Why am I often late for appointments?

Why do I struggle to leave the house on time?

Why do I lose track of time in the mornings?

Why don't I have a consistent morning routine?

Why is my routine not established?

Through this process, you may discover that the root issue is the lack of a structured morning routine. Implementing a consistent routine, such as preparing the night before and setting reminders, can address the problem effectively. This technique helps in pinpointing specific issues and developing targeted solutions.

Overcoming Challenges with Kaizen

While Kaizen emphasizes gradual improvement, it's important to acknowledge that obstacles may arise. Overcoming these challenges requires a thoughtful approach and perseverance.

Patience and Persistence

Kaizen is inherently a long-term strategy. Immediate results are rare; instead, the focus is on consistent, small improvements that accumulate over time. Cultivating patience and maintaining persistence are crucial. Understand that every small step contributes to overall progress, and celebrate these incremental successes to keep motivation high. The journey may be slow, but the compounding effect of these efforts can lead to significant achievements.

Accountability and Support

To enhance your commitment to Kaizen, share your objectives and progress with a supportive network. Involving friends, family, or colleagues can provide encouragement and accountability. Additionally, joining groups or communities with similar goals can offer valuable feedback and motivation. These external sources of support can play a significant role in sustaining your Kaizen efforts and achieving your goals.

Conclusion: The Transformative Power of Kaizen

The philosophy of Kaizen reveals that genuine, lasting improvement emerges from small, consistent efforts. By embracing this approach, we can tackle seemingly daunting goals with a sense of gradual progress. The essence of Kaizen lies in patience, persistence, and a commitment to continuous enhancement. As you integrate Kaizen into your daily life, remember that each small step contributes to a larger journey of personal and professional growth. By adopting this philosophy, you can create a culture of ongoing improvement, leading to meaningful and sustainable success. The transformative power of Kaizen lies in the cumulative impact of each minor effort, ultimately guiding you closer to your objectives and fostering a deeper sense of fulfillment.

CHAPTER 3 THE POMODORO TECHNIQUE

The Pomodoro Technique – Enhancing Productivity

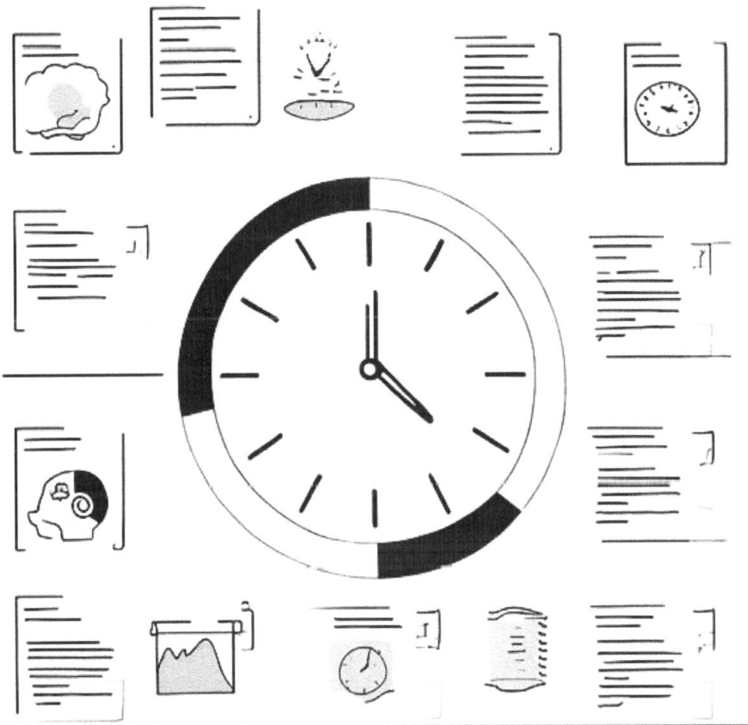

Introduction: Time Management Reimagined

In the modern era of constant distractions and overwhelming workloads, effective time management has become a crucial skill. The Pomodoro Technique offers a simple yet highly effective method to boost productivity and maintain focus. Named after the Italian word for 'tomato,' this technique breaks work into manageable intervals, promoting a balanced rhythm of work and rest.

Imagine a day where you complete your tasks with ease, free from the stress of looming deadlines and endless to-do lists. Picture yourself ending each workday with a sense of accomplishment, having made significant progress on your goals without feeling drained or exhausted. The Pomodoro Technique can turn this vision into reality.

This chapter explores the origins of the Pomodoro Technique, its underlying principles, and practical applications to transform your productivity. Whether you are a student, professional, or someone juggling multiple responsibilities, the Pomodoro Technique offers a versatile approach to time management that can be tailored to fit any lifestyle. Prepare to embark on a journey of discovery as we delve into the fascinating world of the Pomodoro Technique and uncover its potential to revolutionize the way you work.

The Birth of the Pomodoro Technique

The Pomodoro Technique was conceived in the late 1980s by Francesco Cirillo, an Italian university student struggling to stay focused on his studies. Faced with distractions and the challenge of managing his time effectively, Cirillo sought a solution that would allow him to enhance his productivity and concentration. His simple yet revolutionary idea was born from an ordinary kitchen timer shaped like a tomato, or "pomodoro" in Italian.

Cirillo's initial experiment was straightforward: he set the timer for 25 minutes and dedicated this period solely to focused study, followed by a short break. This method proved incredibly effective, and the Pomodoro Technique quickly evolved into a structured approach to time management.

One of the most intriguing aspects of the Pomodoro Technique is its foundation in cognitive psychology. The technique leverages the brain's natural tendency to work in bursts of high energy, known as ultradian rhythms. Research has shown that the human brain can maintain optimal focus for approximately 25-30 minutes before needing a rest to recharge. By aligning work intervals with these natural rhythms, the Pomodoro Technique maximizes productivity and minimizes mental fatigue.

A mind-boggling fact about the Pomodoro Technique is its ability to combat procrastination. Procrastination often stems from the daunting nature of large tasks, which can lead to feelings of overwhelm and avoidance. By breaking tasks into manageable 25-minute intervals, the Pomodoro Technique makes even the most formidable projects seem achievable. This simple shift in perspective can significantly reduce procrastination, allowing individuals to tackle their work with renewed motivation and confidence.

Moreover, the Pomodoro Technique's structured breaks are not merely a respite from work but also an opportunity to refresh the mind. Studies have shown that taking regular breaks can enhance creativity, improve decision-making, and boost overall mental health. The combination of focused work and intentional rest creates a balanced approach to productivity that is both sustainable and effective.

The Pomodoro Technique has transcended its humble beginnings to become a globally recognized time management method. It is now widely used by students, professionals, and creatives alike, each adapting it to their unique needs and workflows. By understanding the origins and scientific principles behind the Pomodoro Technique, we can appreciate its profound impact on productivity and well-being, setting the stage for its practical application in our daily lives.

How the Pomodoro Technique Works

The Pomodoro Technique is straightforward and can be broken down into the following steps:

Choose a Task: Select a task you need to work on.

Set a Timer: Set a timer for 25 minutes, the duration of one Pomodoro.

Work on the Task: Focus solely on the task until the timer rings.

Take a Short Break: Take a 5-minute break to relax.

Repeat: After completing four Pomodoros, take a longer break of 15-30 minutes.

The Science Behind the Pomodoro Technique

Research in cognitive psychology supports the effectiveness of the Pomodoro Technique. Studies have shown that frequent breaks can improve focus, reduce mental fatigue, and enhance overall productivity. According to a study published in the *Journal of Cognitive Neuroscience*, taking short breaks during prolonged tasks can help maintain a high level of performance. The brain's ability to sustain attention diminishes over time, and regular breaks allow it to recover, leading to better performance and productivity.

One fascinating fact is that the brain can only maintain intense focus for about 25 minutes before it starts to wane, which is exactly the interval suggested by the Pomodoro Technique. This aligns perfectly with research from the University of Illinois, which found that brief diversions from a task can dramatically improve one's ability to focus on that task for prolonged periods. This phenomenon, known as the "vigilance decrement," describes how performance declines when we try to maintain attention on a single task for a long time. Short, scheduled breaks help counteract this effect.

Moreover, a study conducted by the Draugiem Group using time-tracking productivity software revealed that the most productive workers took regular breaks, roughly 17 minutes for every 52 minutes of work. These breaks allowed employees to reset, leading to more efficient and creative problem-solving. This discovery is particularly surprising as it challenges the traditional belief that long, uninterrupted work periods are the most productive.

In addition, research by the Association for Psychological Science highlighted the "spacing effect," which indicates that information is better retained when learning sessions are spaced out over time rather than crammed into one session. Applying the Pomodoro Technique not only boosts productivity but also enhances learning and memory retention, making it a powerful tool for both professional and academic settings.

Another intriguing finding comes from the field of occupational health. Studies have shown that regular breaks, as prescribed by the Pomodoro Technique, can reduce the risk of developing musculoskeletal disorders, which are common in professions requiring prolonged periods of sitting or repetitive tasks. By incorporating frequent movement and stretching breaks, individuals can mitigate physical strain and maintain overall health.

These scientific insights underscore the effectiveness of the Pomodoro Technique, revealing how simple, structured intervals of work and rest can optimize cognitive function, productivity, and well-being.

Practical Applications of the Pomodoro Technique

The Pomodoro Technique's strength lies in its simplicity and adaptability. Here’s how you can integrate it effectively into various aspects of your life:

Setting Up Your Pomodoro Workspace

Creating an environment conducive to the Pomodoro Technique is essential for maximizing its benefits. Here are some tips for setting up your workspace:

Minimize Distractions: Turn off notifications on your phone and computer. Inform your colleagues or family members about your work intervals to avoid interruptions. Creating a distraction-free zone allows you to maintain focus and momentum during each Pomodoro.

Organize Your Space: Keep your workspace tidy and free from clutter. A clean and organized environment can improve focus and efficiency. Knowing where everything is located reduces time wasted looking for materials and helps maintain a steady workflow.

Prepare Necessary Tools: Ensure you have all the materials you need before starting a Pomodoro. This includes documents, software, or any other resources related to your task. Having everything at hand prevents interruptions and keeps you immersed in your work.

Comfort and Ergonomics: Make sure your workspace is comfortable and ergonomically sound. A good chair, proper lighting, and a well-positioned desk can help you stay focused and reduce physical strain during extended work sessions.

Integrating the Pomodoro Technique into Daily Life

The Pomodoro Technique can be applied to various aspects of daily life, from professional tasks to personal projects. Here are some practical applications:

Work and Study: Use Pomodoros to manage work tasks or study sessions. Breaking down large projects into smaller intervals makes them more manageable and less daunting. For instance, if you're working on a report, dedicate one Pomodoro to researching, another to outlining, and subsequent Pomodoros to writing and editing.

Household Chores: Apply the technique to household chores by setting a timer for each task. This can make chores feel less overwhelming and more structured. For example, spend one Pomodoro cleaning the kitchen, another organizing the living room, and a third folding laundry. The timer helps turn mundane tasks into timed challenges, making them more engaging.

Creative Pursuits: For creative activities like writing, painting, or music, Pomodoros can help maintain focus and prevent burnout. The breaks provide a moment to recharge and return with fresh inspiration. For instance, use one Pomodoro to brainstorm ideas, another to draft, and a third to refine your work. The structured intervals ensure you make consistent progress while allowing time for creative reflection.

Physical Fitness: The Pomodoro Technique can also be used to structure exercise routines. Set a timer for different workout segments, such as warm-up, cardio, strength training, and cool-down. This method helps you stay on track and ensures a balanced workout.

Learning and Skill Development: Apply Pomodoros to learning new skills or studying new subjects. Whether it's learning a language, mastering a new software tool, or studying for an exam, the technique can help you stay disciplined and make steady progress.

Personal Projects: Whether it's gardening, DIY projects, or any personal hobbies, use Pomodoros to allocate time effectively. This helps in making consistent progress without feeling overwhelmed.

The Benefits of Short Breaks

One of the most surprising benefits of the Pomodoro Technique is the impact of short breaks. Initially, 5-minute breaks may seem insignificant, but they provide essential mental relaxation. These brief moments allow you to stretch, grab a cup of coffee, or simply take a few deep breaths. Over time, these small breaks help to prevent burnout, maintain high energy levels, and enhance overall productivity.

The Pomodoro Technique demonstrates the power of incremental progress and structured time management. By breaking tasks into manageable intervals and incorporating regular breaks, you can enhance your focus, productivity, and overall well-being. Whether applied to work, study, household chores, or creative pursuits, the Pomodoro Technique offers a practical approach to achieving your goals with greater efficiency and less stress. As you integrate this technique into your daily life, you'll discover its potential to transform how you approach tasks and manage your time.

Personal Experience: Mastering the Pomodoro Technique

When I first learned about the Pomodoro Technique, its simplicity made me skeptical. However, eager to enhance my productivity, I decided to give it a try. Initially, I applied it to my work tasks by setting a timer for 25 minutes and focusing solely on the task at hand. It was challenging at first to resist the urge to check emails or social media, but with persistence, I gradually managed to stay focused during these intervals.

One particular instance stands out vividly. I had a major project deadline approaching and felt overwhelmed by the sheer amount of work required. By using the Pomodoro Technique, I broke the project into smaller, more manageable tasks, dedicating specific Pomodoros to each one. This approach not only made the project seem less daunting but also allowed me to track my progress and maintain motivation.

The most surprising benefit came from the breaks. Initially, I doubted that a 5-minute break would make much difference. However, these brief respites provided essential mental relaxation. I used the time to stretch, grab a cup of coffee, or simply take a few deep breaths. These small breaks re-energized me and prepared me for the next Pomodoro session.

Over time, I noticed a significant improvement in my productivity and focus. Tasks that previously took hours to complete were now finished in a fraction of the time. This technique also helped me develop a better work-life balance, as I was able to complete my work more efficiently, leaving more time for personal activities and relaxation.

The Pomodoro Technique wasn't a magic solution that transformed me into a superhuman, but it provided a practical and structured approach to managing my time and tasks. By breaking down work into manageable intervals and incorporating regular breaks, I was able to maintain a steady pace and sustain my energy throughout the day. This method showed me the power of small, consistent efforts and how they can lead to significant improvements over time.

Overcoming Challenges with the Pomodoro Technique

Despite its simplicity, the Pomodoro Technique can present some challenges, particularly in maintaining consistency and dealing with interruptions. Here are some strategies to overcome these challenges:

Staying Consistent

Consistency is key to the success of the Pomodoro Technique. Here are some tips to stay consistent:

Set a Schedule: Plan your Pomodoros in advance. Dedicate specific time blocks each day for focused work.

Track Your Progress: Keep a record of completed Pomodoros. This can provide a sense of accomplishment and motivate you to stay on track.

Adjust as Needed: Be flexible with your approach. If 25 minutes feels too long or too short, adjust the duration to fit your work style.

Managing Interruptions

Interruptions can disrupt your Pomodoros and hinder productivity. Here are some strategies to manage interruptions:

Inform Others: Let your colleagues, friends, or family members know about your Pomodoro intervals and request not to be disturbed during these times.

Use a Signal: Consider using a visible signal, such as a sign or light, to indicate when you are in a Pomodoro session.

Pause and Resume: If an interruption is unavoidable, pause the timer and resume once you can return to focused work.

Conclusion: The Transformative Power of the Pomodoro Technique

The Pomodoro Technique is a simple yet powerful tool for enhancing productivity and focus. By breaking work into manageable intervals and incorporating regular breaks, it helps maintain high levels of performance and prevents burnout. Whether applied to professional tasks, personal projects, or daily chores, the Pomodoro Technique can lead to significant improvements in efficiency and well-being.

As we continue to explore Japanese techniques for life improvement, the Pomodoro Technique stands out as a practical and accessible method for achieving greater productivity and balance. By embracing this technique, you can transform your approach to work and time management, paving the way for a more productive and fulfilling life.

CHAPTER 4 HARA HACHI-BU

Hara Hachi-bu – The Japanese Art of Moderation

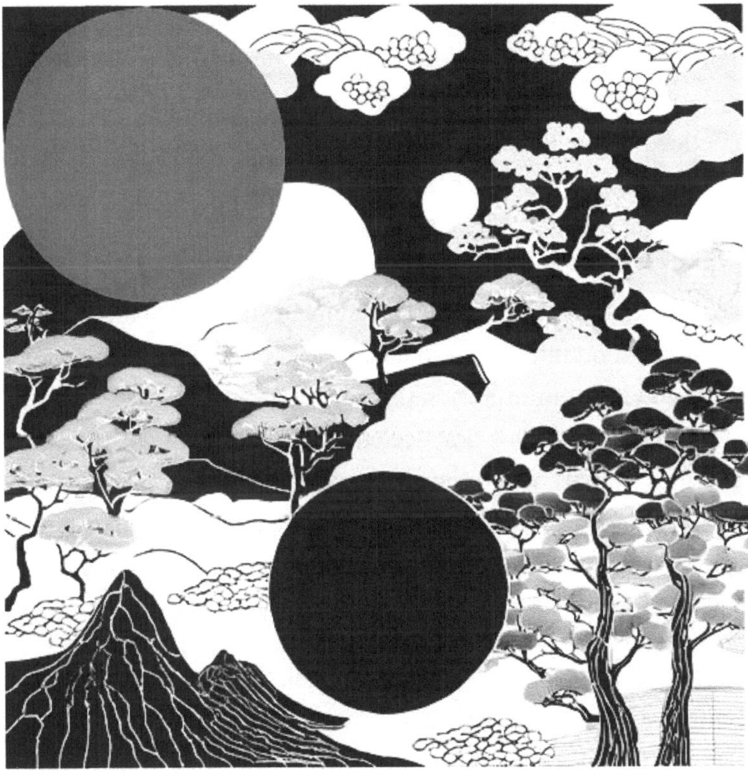

Introduction: The Concept of Hara hachi bu

Hara hachi bu is a principle deeply embedded in Japanese culture, translating to "eat until you are 80% full." This ancient concept transcends mere dietary advice, embodying a broader philosophy of moderation and mindful living. It draws its origins from Confucian teachings, which advocate for balance and self-discipline, and has been practiced by the Okinawans, renowned for their extraordinary longevity and vibrant health.

The Essence of Hara hachi bu

At its core, Hara hachi bu is about achieving a state of balance—not just in terms of food intake, but in how we approach life. The idea is to eat until you are comfortably satisfied, but not so full that you feel uncomfortably stuffed. This practice encourages individuals to listen to their bodies' signals, recognizing the point at which they have had enough. By adhering to this principle, people can enjoy their meals more fully, experience better digestion, and avoid the pitfalls of overconsumption.

The roots of Hara hachi bu can be traced back to Confucian teachings, which emphasize the virtues of moderation and self-control. These teachings have been woven into various aspects of Japanese culture, influencing not only eating habits but also broader lifestyle choices. Confucianism advocates for a balanced approach to life, where excess is avoided, and moderation is practiced. Hara hachi encapsulates these values in a tangible way, offering a practical method for individuals to integrate moderation into their daily routines.

Cultural Significance in Japan

In Japan, where culture often intertwines with practices that promote well-being, Hara hachi bu serves as a subtle yet profound reminder of the benefits of moderation. Japanese culture places a high value on harmony and balance, which are reflected in many aspects of life, including diet. Traditional Japanese meals are characterized by their simplicity and emphasis on seasonal, fresh ingredients, aligning with the principles of moderation.

For the Okinawans, who are known for their longevity and low incidence of age-related diseases, Hara hachi bu is a key component of their lifestyle. The practice of eating until only 80% full is part of a broader set of habits that contribute to their remarkable health. Okinawan meals are often composed of a variety of nutrient-dense foods, consumed in modest portions. This approach to eating helps them maintain a healthy weight and supports their overall well-being.

Mindful Consumption and Lifestyle

Hara hachi bu is not just about how much you eat but also about how you eat. It encourages a mindful approach to consumption, where the act of eating becomes a deliberate and thoughtful experience. By focusing on the taste, texture, and enjoyment of food, individuals can foster a deeper appreciation for their meals and resist the urge to eat out of habit or boredom.

This mindful approach extends beyond eating to other areas of life. The principle of moderation encourages individuals to savor experiences, appreciate the present moment, and avoid overindulgence in various aspects of their lives. Whether it's work, leisure, or personal relationships, Hara hachi bu promotes a balanced approach, helping individuals navigate life's demands with greater ease and satisfaction.

Benefits of Practicing Hara hachi bu

Implementing Hara hachi bu can lead to numerous benefits, both physical and psychological. From a health perspective, eating until you are 80% full helps regulate portion sizes, reducing the risk of overeating and weight gain. It also supports better digestion, as the body has a chance to process food more efficiently without the burden of excessive intake.

Psychologically, Hara hachi bu fosters a sense of contentment and satisfaction with less. By practicing moderation, individuals can experience greater enjoyment from their meals and avoid the discomfort that often accompanies overeating. This sense of fulfillment can extend to other areas of life, creating a harmonious balance that contributes to overall well-being.

Incorporating Hara hachi bu into daily life can also lead to improved mental clarity and focus. By avoiding the sluggishness that can result from overeating, individuals may find themselves more energized and alert throughout the day. This can enhance productivity, creativity, and overall quality of life.

A Holistic Approach to Well-Being

Hara hachi bu embodies a holistic approach to well-being, integrating dietary habits with a broader philosophy of moderation. It serves as a reminder of the importance of balance in all aspects of life, from food and health to personal goals and relationships. By embracing this principle, individuals can cultivate a more mindful and fulfilling lifestyle, enhancing their overall quality of life.

In summary, Hara hachi bu is more than just a dietary practice; it is a reflection of a cultural philosophy that values balance, moderation, and mindful living. By understanding and implementing this principle, individuals can experience a range of benefits that contribute to their physical, mental, and emotional well-being. Whether you are looking to improve your eating habits, enhance your overall health, or simply embrace a more balanced approach to life, Hara hachi bu offers valuable insights and practical guidance for achieving a harmonious and fulfilling existence.

The Origins of Hara hachi bu

Hara hachi bu is not a modern invention but a concept with deep historical roots. Its origins can be traced back to the Confucian teachings that emphasized moderation and balance in all aspects of life. In Okinawa, where this principle is most widely practiced, it has become a cornerstone of the local culture and diet. Okinawans are renowned for their longevity and vibrant health, and Hara hachi bu is believed to play a significant role in their remarkable life expectancy.

This practice is intertwined with the broader philosophy of Ikigai, which seeks to find balance and purpose in life. Hara hachi bu complements this philosophy by promoting moderation in consumption and living in alignment with one's values. It serves as a daily reminder that living well is about more than just avoiding excess—it's about embracing simplicity and appreciating what you have. This alignment between diet and philosophy underscores the deep cultural significance of Hara hachi bu and its role in fostering a balanced and fulfilling life.

The Health Benefits of Hara hachi bu

Adopting the Hara hachi bu principle can have profound effects on physical health. Research has shown that eating until you're 80% full can help in maintaining a healthy weight and reducing the risk of obesity-related conditions such as diabetes and heart disease. This practice encourages mindful eating, which leads to better digestion and a more balanced metabolism.

One significant benefit of Hara hachi bu is its potential impact on longevity. Studies on caloric restriction, which aligns with the principles of Hara hachi bu, suggest that reducing calorie intake without malnutrition can extend lifespan and improve overall health. This is particularly evident in Okinawan populations, who consistently exhibit lower rates of chronic diseases and longer life spans compared to other populations. By avoiding overconsumption and focusing on moderation, individuals can enhance their well-being and potentially extend their years of healthy living.

Furthermore, Hara hachi bu promotes a healthier relationship with food. By eating mindfully and recognizing when you're satisfied, you develop a greater appreciation for the flavors and textures of your meals. This mindful approach to eating can lead to improved mental health and reduced stress, as the focus shifts from consumption to enjoyment. Embracing Hara hachi bu encourages individuals to savor their food and appreciate the nourishment it provides, contributing to overall well-being and satisfaction.

Applying Hara hachi bu in Daily Life

Incorporating Hara hachi bu into your daily routine involves more than just adjusting portion sizes; it requires a shift in mindset towards mindful eating and moderation. Here are some practical steps to apply Hara hachi bu in your life:

Mindful Eating: Start by paying attention to your hunger cues. Eat slowly and savor each bite, recognizing when you begin to feel satisfied. This practice not only enhances your eating experience but also helps prevent overeating.

Portion Control: Use smaller plates and bowls to naturally limit portion sizes. By serving yourself smaller amounts, you're less likely to overeat and can more easily adhere to the 80% full principle.

Healthy Choices: Opt for nutrient-dense foods that provide greater satisfaction with smaller quantities. Incorporate a variety of vegetables, fruits, lean proteins, and whole grains into your meals to ensure balanced nutrition.

Regular Meals: Maintain regular meal times and avoid skipping meals. Eating consistently throughout the day helps regulate appetite and prevents excessive hunger, which can lead to overeating.

Listening to Your Body: Tune into your body's signals and eat based on true hunger rather than emotional triggers or external cues. This approach helps establish a healthier relationship with food and promotes a balanced diet.

By integrating these practices into your daily routine, you can embrace the principles of Hara hachi bu and enjoy the numerous benefits of moderation and mindful eating. This approach not only supports physical health but also fosters a greater sense of overall well-being and satisfaction in your life.

Hara hachi bu in the Context of Modern Living

In today's fast-paced world, where convenience often takes precedence over mindfulness, incorporating Hara hachi bu can serve as a refreshing reminder to slow down and appreciate the simple pleasures of life. The modern lifestyle, marked by constant hustle, high-calorie, processed foods, and a culture of instant gratification, can make it challenging to practice moderation. However, the principles of Hara hachi bu offer a valuable counterbalance to this trend, encouraging a more mindful and intentional approach to both eating and living.

The Challenge of Modern Living

Modern life presents numerous challenges to the practice of moderation. The prevalence of fast food and processed snacks, combined with the demands of busy schedules, often leads to hurried meals and mindless eating. People frequently eat on the go, in front of screens, or while multitasking, which can diminish their awareness of hunger and fullness cues. This environment makes it easy to fall into the trap of overeating, as portion sizes increase and the quality of food decreases.

Moreover, the pressure to keep up with a relentless pace of work and social commitments can leave little room for self-care and reflection. In this context, the idea of eating until you are only 80% full may seem impractical or challenging. Yet, integrating Hara hachi bu into daily life offers a pathway to reclaiming balance and mindfulness amidst the chaos.

Strategies for Adapting Hara hachi bu

To incorporate Hara hachi bu into modern living effectively, consider the following strategies that align with contemporary lifestyles while honoring traditional principles:

1. Mindful Eating Practices

Mindful eating involves focusing on the sensory experience of eating, which can help reinforce the principles of Hara hachi bu. Here are some practical tips:

Eat Without Distractions: Set aside dedicated time for meals where you are not distracted by phones, computers, or television. This allows you to fully engage with the experience of eating and tune into your body's signals.

Chew Thoroughly: Take time to chew each bite thoroughly, savoring the flavors and textures of your food. This practice not only enhances your enjoyment but also aids digestion and helps you recognize when you're reaching the 80% full mark.

Be Present During Meals: Practice being present during meals by paying attention to the taste, smell, and appearance of your food. Engage in conversations about the food and its origins, which can deepen your appreciation and mindfulness.

2. Healthy Meal Planning

Planning and preparing meals in advance can help you adhere to Hara hachi bu principles and avoid the pitfalls of convenience foods. Consider the following:

Plan Balanced Meals: Develop a weekly meal plan that includes a variety of fresh, whole ingredients. Aim to balance your meals with vegetables, lean proteins, whole grains, and healthy fats. Portion control is key—serve yourself appropriate portions to align with the 80% full principle.

Prepare in Advance: Batch cook meals or prepare components of meals ahead of time. Having healthy options readily available can reduce the temptation to reach for processed or unhealthy foods when you're short on time.

Portion Control: Use smaller plates and bowls to help regulate portion sizes. This visual cue can help you avoid overeating and make it easier to stop eating when you're 80% full.

3. Work-Life Balance

Applying the concept of moderation to other areas of life can enhance your overall well-being:

Balance Productivity and Relaxation: Strive to maintain a balanced approach to work and leisure. Allocate time for relaxation and self-care, and avoid overworking or sacrificing personal time for professional demands.

Set Boundaries: Establish clear boundaries between work and personal life. Create designated times for work and leisure activities, ensuring that you have dedicated moments to unwind and recharge.

Prioritize Self-Care: Engage in activities that promote mental and emotional well-being, such as exercise, hobbies, or spending time with loved ones. A balanced lifestyle contributes to a greater sense of fulfillment and reduces stress.

4. Cultural Adaptation

Embracing cultural aspects of Hara hachi bu can deepen your connection to the principles of moderation and mindfulness:

Explore Traditional Dining Practices: Familiarize yourself with traditional Japanese dining customs, such as eating with chopsticks, which encourages slower eating and portion control. Pay attention to the presentation and variety of foods, which reflect the principles of balance and harmony.

Appreciate Meal Presentation: Take time to appreciate the aesthetics of your meals. Traditional Japanese cuisine often emphasizes the visual appeal of dishes, highlighting the importance of presentation and portion control.

Incorporate Cultural Mindfulness: Integrate elements of Japanese mindfulness into your eating habits, such as expressing gratitude for your meal and being aware of the cultural significance of different foods.

Embracing Hara hachi bu in Modern Times

Integrating Hara hachi bu into your modern lifestyle is not just about adhering to a dietary principle but about fostering a broader mindset of moderation and mindfulness. By adopting these strategies, you can create a more balanced and fulfilling approach to eating and living. The practice of eating until you are 80% full can serve as a valuable tool for managing portion sizes, enhancing enjoyment, and promoting overall well-being.

The Benefits of a Mindful Approach

Embracing Hara hachi bu offers numerous benefits beyond just improved digestion and weight management. It encourages a more mindful and intentional approach to life, fostering greater appreciation for the simple pleasures and helping to combat the negative effects of overconsumption and stress. By integrating these practices into your daily routine, you can achieve a harmonious balance that supports both physical and mental health.

In conclusion, Hara hachi bu provides a timeless principle for modern living, offering a pathway to mindfulness, balance, and well-being. By adapting this ancient wisdom to contemporary life, you can enjoy the benefits of moderation and create a more fulfilling and harmonious lifestyle. The journey towards mindful living begins with small, deliberate steps, and embracing Hara hachi bu can be a powerful first step in that journey.

Conclusion: The Legacy of Hara hachi bu

Hara hachi bu, with its roots in ancient Confucian teachings and its prominence in Okinawan culture, offers a timeless and valuable lesson in moderation. This principle, advocating for eating until you're 80% full, embodies a broader philosophy of balance and mindful living. By embracing Hara hachi bu, individuals can enhance their physical health, cultivate a healthier relationship with food, and find greater satisfaction in life.

As we navigate the complexities of modern living, the wisdom of Hara hachi bu serves as a gentle reminder of the importance of moderation and mindfulness. By integrating this principle into our daily lives, we can achieve a harmonious balance between consumption and well-being, ultimately leading to a more fulfilling and enriched existence. Embracing Hara hachi bu not only supports physical health but also fosters a deeper appreciation for the simple pleasures of life, encouraging us to live with intention and gratitude.

CHAPTER 5 EMBRACING MINIMALISM

Embracing Minimalism – The Japanese Art of Decluttering

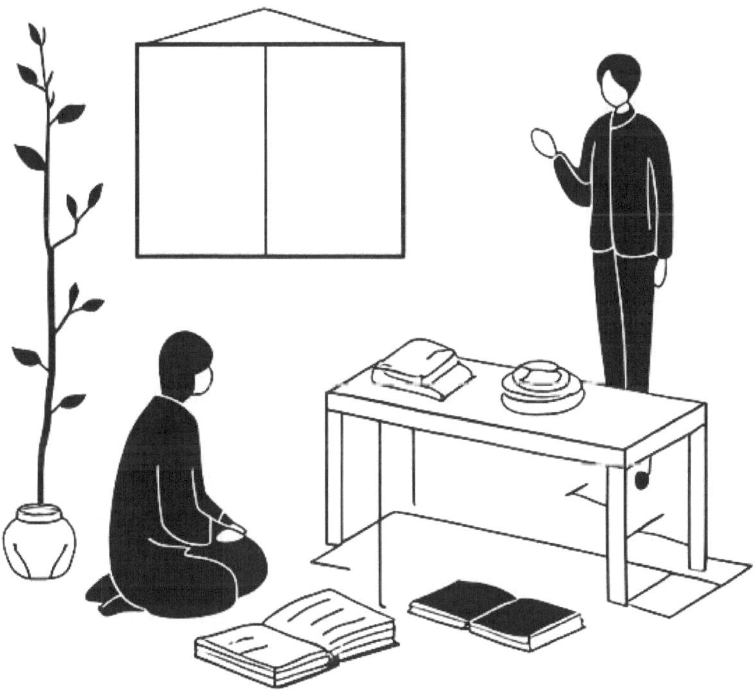

Introduction: The Concept of Shoshin

Shoshin, often translated as "Beginner's Mind," is a profound concept deeply rooted in Zen Buddhism and traditional Japanese culture. This principle advocates approaching life with a fresh perspective, characterized by openness, curiosity, and humility. It encourages individuals to view each experience, task, or interaction as if they were encountering it for the first time, free from preconceived notions and biases.

At its core, Shoshin embodies the spirit of constant learning and personal growth. It invites us to shed the weight of accumulated knowledge and experience, which often leads to rigid thinking and complacency. Instead, it fosters a mindset of wonder and exploration, where each moment is approached with a sense of wonder and eagerness to discover something new. This approach not only enriches our understanding but also deepens our engagement with life.

In the realm of minimalism and decluttering, Shoshin offers a particularly valuable perspective. The principles of minimalism emphasize simplicity and intentional living, urging us to pare down our lives to what is truly meaningful and necessary. When combined with the Shoshin mindset, this approach becomes even more powerful. By adopting a beginner's mind, we challenge ourselves to reevaluate our possessions, habits, and daily routines without the constraints of past experiences or societal expectations.

Applying Shoshin to minimalism means looking at our environment and belongings as if we are seeing them for the first time. This fresh perspective can be transformative, encouraging us to let go of items that no longer serve a purpose and to appreciate the true value of what remains. It invites us to question our attachments to material possessions and to focus on what truly brings us joy and fulfillment.

For instance, when decluttering our living spaces, Shoshin encourages us to examine each item with a sense of curiosity and openness. Instead of simply discarding things out of habit or routine, we ask ourselves whether they genuinely contribute to our well-being and happiness. This mindset shift can lead to a more intentional approach to consumption, where we make thoughtful decisions about what to keep and what to let go.

Shoshin also plays a significant role in cultivating a minimalist mindset by helping us appreciate the beauty and value in simplicity. It teaches us to find joy in the essentials and to recognize that less can indeed be more. By approaching our daily lives with a beginner's mind, we can embrace the art of simplicity and create a more harmonious and balanced existence.

Ultimately, the concept of Shoshin offers a pathway to deeper fulfillment through minimalism. It encourages us to embrace each moment with fresh eyes, to let go of excess, and to find contentment in the simple pleasures of life. By integrating Shoshin into our minimalist journey, we can foster a greater appreciation for simplicity and cultivate a more meaningful and purposeful life.

Shoshin in the Context of Modern Living

In our modern, consumer-driven society, the principle of Shoshin —"Beginner's Mind"—offers a refreshing antidote to the overwhelming clutter and complexity that characterize contemporary life. Today's world is inundated with marketing messages, societal pressures, and a culture that often prioritizes excess over necessity. This environment makes it all too easy to accumulate more possessions and distractions than we truly need, leading us to lose sight of what genuinely matters.

Shoshin encourages us to take a step back and view our lives from a fresh perspective, free from the biases and attachments that cloud our judgment. This approach allows us to critically assess the value of our belongings, habits, and routines, leading to a more intentional and fulfilling way of living. By adopting a beginner's mindset, we can challenge the norms of consumerism and rediscover what truly enriches our lives.

Applying Shoshin to Minimalism

Integrating Shoshin into your minimalist journey involves several key strategies:

Adopt a Fresh Perspective: Start by approaching your possessions and living space as if you are encountering them for the first time. This fresh outlook helps you objectively evaluate what truly contributes to your well-being. For instance, if you were to view your living space anew, you might realize that certain items, once considered valuable, no longer align with your current needs or values. This perspective shift can make it easier to identify and let go of possessions that no longer serve a purpose in your life.

Let Go of Attachments: Shoshin teaches us to release our emotional attachments to material possessions. By applying a beginner's mind to the decluttering process, you can assess each item without the usual sentimental biases. This approach allows you to make more rational decisions about what to keep and what to discard. For example, if you find yourself holding on to clothing that no longer fits or is out of style simply because it reminds you of past experiences, Shoshin encourages you to evaluate its current value rather than its sentimental history.

Embrace the Joy of Simplicity: Minimalism is not just about reducing the number of items you own but also about finding joy in simplicity. Shoshin encourages you to rediscover the pleasure in a well-organized space and a few meaningful possessions. This might involve appreciating the beauty of a clean, uncluttered room or the serenity that comes from having a few carefully chosen items that truly enhance your life. By focusing on the essentials, you can experience greater satisfaction and contentment with less.

Cultivate Curiosity: Approach your decluttering efforts with curiosity and an open mind. Explore innovative ways to organize your space, simplify your belongings, and enhance your living environment. For instance, you might experiment with different storage solutions or embrace new organizational systems that you haven't tried before. This mindset helps you see opportunities for improvement and fosters a deeper appreciation for the minimalist lifestyle. By viewing decluttering as an ongoing journey of discovery, you can continually refine and enhance your living space.

Practice Mindful Consumption: Use the principles of Shoshin to guide your purchasing decisions. Before acquiring new items, ask yourself whether they genuinely add value to your life or simply contribute to clutter. This mindful approach helps prevent unnecessary accumulation and promotes a more intentional lifestyle. For example, before making a purchase, consider if the item will truly enhance your daily life or if it is an impulse buy driven by external pressures or fleeting desires.

By integrating these strategies into your minimalist journey, Shoshin can help you cultivate a more intentional and fulfilling lifestyle. It offers a transformative approach to decluttering and minimalism, enabling you to find greater satisfaction and joy in simplicity. Embracing the beginner's mind allows you to reassess your possessions and habits with a fresh perspective, leading to a more balanced and meaningful life.

Practical Applications of Shoshin in Decluttering

Creating a Minimalist Workspace

Applying the principle of Shoshin, or "Beginner's Mind," to your workspace can yield significant benefits in productivity, creativity, and overall well-being. A minimalist workspace, free from clutter, not only promotes a clearer mind but also enhances focus and efficiency. Here's how to transform your workspace using Shoshin:

Start with a Clean Slate:

Begin by clearing everything off your desk or workspace. This blank canvas allows you to view your environment with fresh eyes, akin to a beginner seeing something for the first time. As you remove each item, take a moment to appreciate the empty space and envision how it can be utilized more effectively. This process helps you understand what truly needs to be on your desk and what might be adding unnecessary clutter.

Organize by Function:

Once your workspace is clear, start placing items back based on their function and importance. Focus on keeping only the essentials within reach. Frequently used tools, such as a computer, notepad, or pens, should be easily accessible, while less critical items can be stored out of sight. This functional organization not only reduces clutter but also enhances efficiency by ensuring that everything you need is within easy reach. For instance, if you frequently refer to reference materials, consider using a vertical file organizer to keep them easily accessible yet out of the way.

Implement Minimalist Design Principles:

Adopting minimalist design principles can help create a visually appealing and functional workspace. Opt for clean lines, simple colors, and functional furnishings. Choose a desk with ample surface area but minimalistic design, and use storage solutions that blend seamlessly into the space. For example, a sleek, white desk with built-in drawers keeps your essentials organized while maintaining a clean look. Use neutral colors and simple decor to create a calm and focused environment. Avoid ornate or distracting decorations that might detract from your work.

Regular Maintenance:

Maintaining a minimalist workspace requires regular attention. Schedule periodic decluttering sessions to ensure that only necessary items remain. This practice helps you stay organized and adapt to any changes in your work requirements. For instance, set aside time each month to review your workspace and remove items that are no longer needed. This ongoing maintenance keeps your environment fresh and aligned with your productivity goals.

Applying Shoshin to Digital Decluttering

In addition to physical spaces, Shoshin can be applied to digital environments, which often become cluttered with files, emails, and apps. Here's how to implement Shoshin principles in digital decluttering:

Reevaluate Your Digital Tools:

Approach your digital tools and applications as if you're encountering them for the first time. Assess their relevance and usefulness with a fresh perspective. Identify which apps, software, or online tools you truly need and which ones have become obsolete. For example, if you have multiple task management apps, consider consolidating to a single tool that best meets your needs.

Organize Digital Files:

Apply Shoshin to your digital files by organizing them into clear, functional categories. Create a streamlined folder structure that makes it easy to locate and manage your documents. For instance, use broad categories such as "Work," "Personal," and "Projects," and further subdivide these into more specific folders. Regularly review and delete files that are no longer needed to keep your digital space uncluttered.

Clean Up Your Email Inbox:

View your email inbox with a beginner's mind. Start by unsubscribing from newsletters and promotional emails that no longer interest you. Implement a system for categorizing and prioritizing emails, such as using labels or folders. This approach helps you manage your inbox efficiently and prevents it from becoming an overwhelming source of clutter.

Streamline Your Digital Workflows:

Evaluate your digital workflows and tools to ensure they are as efficient as possible. Look for opportunities to simplify processes and eliminate unnecessary steps. For example, if you use multiple communication platforms, consider consolidating to one that integrates with your other tools. This streamlined approach reduces complexity and enhances productivity.

Integrating Shoshin into Personal Spaces

Shoshin can also be applied to personal spaces, such as your home, to create a more intentional and serene environment. Here's how to incorporate this mindset into your personal living spaces:

Reassess Your Home's Layout:

View your home's layout with a fresh perspective. Consider how each room and piece of furniture contributes to your overall living experience. Rearrange furniture and decor to create a more functional and harmonious space. For instance, if a room feels cramped, try reconfiguring the layout to improve flow and make the space feel more open.

Evaluate Your Personal Belongings:

Approach your personal belongings as if you are seeing them for the first time. Assess each item's value and relevance to your current life. This perspective helps you let go of items that no longer serve a purpose or bring you joy. For example, if you have a collection of sentimental items that have become clutter, evaluate their current significance and consider whether they still align with your values.

Create Zones of Calm:

Designate specific areas in your home as zones of calm and relaxation. Apply minimalist principles to these spaces to create a peaceful retreat. For example, set up a reading nook with a comfortable chair, a small table, and a few carefully chosen books. This designated space allows you to unwind and enjoy moments of tranquility amidst your busy life.

Adopt Minimalist Decor:

Choose decor and furnishings that align with minimalist principles. Opt for simple, functional pieces that enhance your living space without creating visual clutter. For example, select a few well-designed items, such as a statement lamp or a piece of art, to add character to your space without overwhelming it.

By applying Shoshin to various aspects of your life, from your workspace to your personal spaces and digital environments, you can create a more intentional and fulfilling lifestyle. This approach encourages you to view your surroundings with fresh eyes, leading to a more organized, serene, and purposeful life.

Applying Shoshin to Personal Belongings

Decluttering your personal belongings with a beginner's mind involves more than just removing excess items. It's about reassessing the value of what you own and making intentional choices about what to keep. Here's a practical approach:

1. **Categorize and Simplify**: Begin by categorizing your belongings into groups such as clothing, books, and electronics. Evaluate each category with a fresh perspective, asking yourself whether each item truly serves a purpose or brings you joy.

2. **Ask the Right Questions**: When evaluating items, ask yourself questions such as:

o Does this item enhance my life?

o Is it used regularly?

o Does it contribute to my sense of well-being?

1. **Focus on Quality Over Quantity**: Embrace the concept of quality over quantity. Invest in fewer, higher-quality items that serve multiple purposes or bring you genuine satisfaction.

2. **Practice Mindful Disposal**: When letting go of items, do so mindfully. Donate, recycle, or repurpose belongings in a way that aligns with your values and minimizes environmental impact.

The Psychological Impact of Shoshin and Minimalism

The psychological benefits of adopting Shoshin and practicing minimalism are profound. Embracing a beginner's mind and simplifying your life can lead to increased mental clarity, reduced stress, and a greater sense of contentment.

Enhanced Mental Clarity

A minimalist environment reduces cognitive overload by minimizing visual and sensory distractions. With fewer possessions and a more organized space, you can experience greater mental clarity and focus on what truly matters.

Reduced Stress and Anxiety

Clutter and excess can contribute to feelings of stress and anxiety. By embracing minimalism and Shoshin, you create a more serene and orderly environment, which can lead to reduced stress and improved emotional well-being.

Increased Sense of Contentment

Simplifying your life and letting go of excess can foster a greater sense of contentment. By focusing on what truly adds value to your life, you can cultivate a deeper appreciation for the simple pleasures and experiences that bring joy and fulfillment.

Real-Life Examples and Quotes

1. **Marie Kondo**: The renowned author and decluttering expert Marie Kondo advocates for the joy of simplicity. Her philosophy of only keeping items that "spark joy" aligns with the principles of Shoshin and minimalism, emphasizing the value of a fresh perspective and intentional living.

2. **William Morris**: The British designer and writer William Morris famously said, "Have nothing in your houses that you do not know to be useful or believe to be beautiful." This quote reflects the essence of Shoshin and minimalism, encouraging us to reevaluate our possessions and embrace simplicity.

3. **Steve Jobs**: The late co-founder of Apple Inc., Steve Jobs, was known for his minimalist approach to design and life. His emphasis on simplicity and focus serves as a powerful example of how a beginner's mind can lead to innovation and excellence.

Conclusion: The Transformative Power of Shoshin and Minimalism

Incorporating Shoshin and minimalism into your life can be a transformative journey. By embracing a beginner's mind, you open yourself to new possibilities, simplify your surroundings, and cultivate a more intentional and fulfilling life. This approach not only enhances your physical environment but also nurtures your mental and emotional well-being.

As you explore the principles of Shoshin and minimalism, remember that the path to simplicity is a continuous process of growth and discovery. Each step you take towards a more mindful and clutter-free life brings you closer to a state of balance and contentment. Embrace the power of Shoshin, and let it guide you towards a life of purpose, clarity, and joy.

CHAPTER 6 WABI-SABI

Wabi-Sabi — Embracing Imperfection

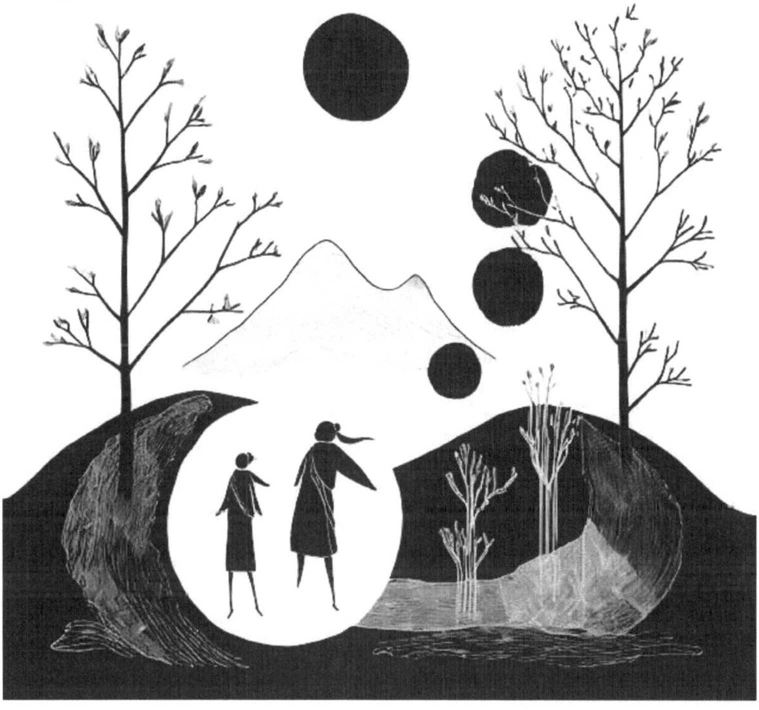

Introduction: The Concept of Wabi-Sabi

Wabi-Sabi is a traditional Japanese aesthetic and philosophical concept that celebrates the beauty of imperfection, impermanence, and incompleteness. Derived from Zen Buddhism, Wabi-Sabi encourages a deep appreciation for the natural cycle of growth and decay, recognizing beauty in simplicity and the humble, unrefined aspects of life.

The term "Wabi" originally referred to the loneliness of living in nature, but over time it evolved to signify a rustic, simple elegance. "Sabi" refers to the beauty that comes with age and wear. Together, Wabi-Sabi embodies an appreciation for the transient and imperfect nature of the world, suggesting that true beauty is found in the fleeting and the unfinished. This concept contrasts sharply with modern standards of perfection, which often emphasize flawlessness and uniformity. Wabi-Sabi invites us to find beauty in the worn and weathered, to value the authentic over the artificial.

In the context of minimalism and decluttering, Wabi-Sabi offers a refreshing perspective. It encourages us to embrace the imperfect nature of our possessions and ourselves, fostering a sense of peace and acceptance. By understanding and applying Wabi-Sabi principles, we can cultivate a more meaningful and contented approach to our lives and our belongings.

Wabi-Sabi in the Context of Modern Living

In an age dominated by consumerism and a relentless pursuit of perfection, Wabi-Sabi serves as a counterbalance, offering a path to tranquility and authenticity. Modern living often promotes the idea that happiness and success are tied to acquiring the latest trends or achieving flawless conditions. However, this constant striving for perfection can lead to dissatisfaction and burnout.

Wabi-Sabi encourages us to shift our focus from the pursuit of perfection to an appreciation of the imperfect and transient. This approach can be particularly valuable in managing the clutter and chaos that often accompany contemporary lifestyles. By embracing Wabi-Sabi, we can learn to appreciate the natural imperfections of our environment and our lives, fostering a more relaxed and mindful approach to daily living.

To integrate Wabi-Sabi into modern living, consider the following strategies:

1. **Redefine Your Standards of Beauty:** Move away from conventional ideals of perfection and find beauty in the unique and imperfect aspects of your life and surroundings. This could mean appreciating the patina on an old piece of furniture or the unique character of a well-loved item.

2. **Accept and Embrace Change:** Recognize that impermanence is a natural part of life. Rather than resisting change or trying to maintain perfect conditions, accept the natural wear and tear that comes with time. This acceptance can bring a sense of peace and reduce stress associated with maintaining an idealized state.

3. **Simplify and Slow Down:** Embrace a minimalist approach that values quality over quantity and finds contentment in

simplicity. This could involve decluttering your home to make space for the things that truly matter, or adopting a slower pace of life that allows you to savor each moment.

4. **Cultivate Mindfulness:** Practice mindfulness to enhance your appreciation of the present moment. By being fully present, you can better appreciate the subtleties and imperfections in your environment and your experiences.

5. **Create a Wabi-Sabi-Inspired Space:** Design a living space that reflects Wabi-Sabi principles by incorporating natural materials, simple designs, and elements that show signs of wear. This can create a calming and aesthetically pleasing environment that celebrates the beauty of imperfection.

Practical Applications of Wabi-Sabi in Decluttering

Embracing Wabi-Sabi in your decluttering process can lead to a more intentional and fulfilling approach. Here are some practical applications:

1. **Reevaluate Your Belongings:** Assess your possessions with a Wabi-Sabi mindset. Rather than focusing on their flaws, consider their history, uniqueness, and the role they play in your life. This perspective can help you make more meaningful decisions about what to keep and what to let go.

2. **Focus on Functionality and Authenticity:** When decluttering, prioritize items that serve a purpose or hold sentimental value. Emphasize functionality and authenticity over aesthetics or trends. This approach can help you maintain a more meaningful and less cluttered living space.

3. **Find Joy in the Imperfect:** Celebrate the imperfections in your possessions and your home. This could involve embracing the cracks in a cherished vase or the worn edges of a favorite book. Recognize that these imperfections add character and history, enhancing the overall beauty of your space.

4. **Practice Gratitude and Acceptance:** Develop a sense of gratitude for the items you choose to keep and the space you create. Accept that no space or object will be perfect and that this imperfection is part of what makes it special. This mindset can reduce the pressure to achieve an idealized standard and foster a greater sense of contentment.

5. **Incorporate Wabi-Sabi in Daily Life:** Extend Wabi-Sabi principles beyond decluttering to other aspects of your life. Embrace the imperfections in your daily routines, relationships, and personal growth. By adopting a more forgiving and accepting attitude, you can create a more balanced and satisfying life.

Real-Life Examples of Wabi-Sabi

Wabi-Sabi has influenced various aspects of Japanese culture and design. Here are some real-life examples that illustrate its application:

1. **Japanese Tea Ceremonies:** Traditional Japanese tea ceremonies embrace Wabi-Sabi by focusing on simplicity, natural materials, and the beauty of imperfection. The tea utensils used in these ceremonies often show signs of wear and

aging, reflecting their history and the appreciation of their unique characteristics.

2. **Kintsugi:** Kintsugi is the Japanese art of repairing broken pottery with lacquer mixed with powdered gold, silver, or platinum. Rather than hiding the cracks, Kintsugi highlights them, celebrating the object's history and imperfections. This practice embodies Wabi-Sabi by transforming damage into a feature of beauty.

3. **Traditional Japanese Gardens:** Japanese gardens often incorporate elements that reflect Wabi-Sabi principles, such as moss-covered stones, weathered wooden structures, and irregularly shaped pathways. These design choices create a harmonious and serene environment that celebrates the natural aging process and the beauty of imperfection.

4. **Wabi-Sabi Architecture:** Traditional Japanese architecture often features simple, natural materials and design elements that age gracefully over time. Buildings are designed to blend seamlessly with their surroundings and to show signs of wear and change, reflecting the Wabi-Sabi appreciation for impermanence and authenticity.

By exploring these examples and integrating Wabi-Sabi principles into your own life, you can cultivate a deeper appreciation for the beauty of imperfection and impermanence. Embracing Wabi-Sabi can lead to a more meaningful and fulfilling approach to both decluttering and everyday living.

Conclusion: The Timeless Beauty of Wabi-Sabi

Embracing Wabi-Sabi invites us to see the world through a lens of acceptance and appreciation for imperfection, impermanence, and incompleteness. In a society often driven by the pursuit of perfection, Wabi-Sabi offers a refreshing and liberating perspective that celebrates the beauty of the natural cycle of growth and decay. By applying Wabi-Sabi principles to our lives, we can cultivate a sense of peace and contentment, finding value in simplicity, authenticity, and the imperfect.

Incorporating Wabi-Sabi into our daily lives encourages us to redefine our standards of beauty, to appreciate the unique characteristics of our possessions, and to accept the inevitable changes that time brings. It teaches us to slow down, simplify, and find joy in the present moment. Whether through decluttering our spaces, reimagining our living environments, or approaching our personal growth with a more forgiving attitude, Wabi-Sabi offers a path to a more balanced, mindful, and fulfilling life.

As you move forward, consider how the principles of Wabi-Sabi can enrich your own journey. By embracing imperfection and celebrating the beauty of the transient, you can create a life that is not only more meaningful but also more aligned with the natural rhythms of the world around you. In this way, Wabi-Sabi becomes not just an aesthetic choice, but a way of life that fosters a deeper connection with yourself and your surroundings.